Contents

Chapter 1 An exciting announcement

It is Monday morning.

On a small Scottish island some children are waiting for the ferry to secondary school. It is raining and the ferry is late. As they wait a man passes them on his bike.

"Hello, Donald!" they call.

"Hello, Rory, Andrew, Neil, Fiona. Have you seen Hamish today?"

"No!" say the children.

"Did he go away again?" asks Fiona.

"Yes," says Donald, "he has been gone for weeks. Someone saw him near the ferry."

"Maybe he is shopping in Portree," says Neil.

Donald and the children all laugh because Hamish is Donald's parrot.

Far away in Glasgow, Primary 6 are learning maths. They are quiet today. It is raining outside and the sky is grey.

Cameron Campbell is sitting next to his friend Louise Smith in the back row. They are both working through a page of maths questions. The maths questions are not very hard and not very interesting.

There is a loud knock on the classroom door. Everyone turns to look at the door. Then the teacher, Mrs MacDonald, calls "Come in."

The door opens slowly. The whole class hopes it will be someone really exciting – like Santa Claus or David Beckham. It is not! It is the head teacher, Mrs McCracken.

She stands in the door and looks around at the quiet class. She looks at the teacher too.

"Mrs MacDonald," she says, "Primary 6, I have an important announcement to make!"

Everyone looks at her.

They wonder what she is going to announce.

One day in Primary 4 she announced that the Prime Minister was coming to the school. One winter she announced that everyone had to go home because it was too cold.

The whole class hopes the announcement will be an exciting one.

It is!

She announces a school trip.

"This is a very special school trip," she tells them. "It is a trip to an outdoor centre. All the children will stay for a week. They can go canoeing, orienteering, abseiling, sailing and kayaking."

It is a trip only for boys and girls who are ten or eleven years old. All Mrs MacDonald's class may go. The school has money to send them on the trip.

Kirsty puts her hand up. "Yes, Kirsty?" asks Mrs McCracken.

"What is the difference between sailing and abseiling?" asks Kirsty. Everyone wants to know this. Kirsty is the only one who asks.

Mrs McCracken tells them that abseiling is a quick way to come down a cliff. You lie down at the end of a rope and walk down the cliff.

She also tells the class more about the trip. The children are all going to Raasay.

Raasay is a small island. It is between the Scottish mainland and Skye (which is a big island next to the Scottish mainland). Everyone has heard of Skye but no one has heard of Raasay.

They will get to the island by bus and by ferry. They will stay in a big house, Raasay House. They will sleep and eat there together. Raasay House has special teachers called "instructors" to help them learn sailing, canoeing and the other things. Every morning they will be taken out to do exciting things. She says a letter will be sent to the parents giving more information soon.

Then she says goodbye to the class. "Good-bye-Miss-us-Mac-Crack-en," the class says and she goes away.

When she has gone Mrs MacDonald stops teaching maths. Everyone is far too excited. They all talk about the trip. For many children it will be their first trip away from home without one of their parents.

In the back row Cameron and Louise are talking in whispers.

"No maths for a week," says Cameron.

"I want to try canoeing," says Louise.

"So do I," says Cameron, "and abseiling."

Chapter 2 Writing about Raasay

It is the week before Primary 6 goes to Raasay. The teacher asks the whole class to do some work about Raasay. She wants them to find out about the island and the holiday. She puts up a special table in the classroom. There are lots of books and maps to work from and a computer. She tells them to use the Internet. She wants every child to write a whole A 4 page about the island, the outdoor centre and the activities there.

Louise is at the table looking at the books. She has already written two pages.

Louise thinks Raasay House is very interesting. She is excited about the trip and she looks at all the books. She wants to know all about it. She has looked on the Internet and read all about the island. She already knows that the name means *Island of Deer*. She has read that most people who live on the island are fishermen or work on Skye. She knows that there is no secondary school on the island and bigger children go to Portree, the capital of Skye, to school.

Cameron does not feel like this. "I really don't want to write about it," he says to her. "I just want to go. I don't want to read about it. I don't want to write about it. I just want to do it."

Louise thinks he is lazy.

"Don't you want to know something about Raasay?" she asks.

"No, I don't!" says Cameron, "I just want to go."

He sits down near her. There are lots of books and some maps. Mrs MacDonald has put a big picture of Raasay House

on the wall over the table. There is also a map of Scotland with a big arrow to show where Raasay is.

Louise pushes some books towards Cameron.

"Here," she says, "look at these. They are good."

Cameron starts to look at one of the books. It is all about Bonnie Prince Charlie.

"You have heard of Bonnie Prince Charlie haven't you?" says Louise.

"Who is he?" says Cameron. "Is he dead? Or is he the Queen's son?"

Louise looks fed up. She looks away and starts to write again. "Raasay has many interesting rocks ...," she writes.

Cameron opens a different book and reads it out loud. "The island of Raasay is 14 miles long and 3 miles wide."

"Could you read that in your head please?" says Louise.

Cameron writes it down at the top of his piece of paper. Then he opens the map of Scotland. It is very big and the table is too small. He can see Aberdeen and Inverness. He cannot see Skye, Raasay or Raasay House. Cameron looks at Louise. Maybe she will help him. She shakes her head and goes back to writing.

Cameron tries to put the map away again, but it will not go. It is not very tidy and it is much bigger than when he started.

Now Cameron turns on the computer to look for the outdoor centre. It is easy to find the website and there are colour pictures as well as a list of activities you can do there.

Climbing and abseiling

Kayaking

Open canoeing

Sailing

This is getting better

He follows the links and looks at the pictures. *Open canoeing* sounds good.

There is a picture of a long narrow boat with two people sitting in it, one at the front and one at the back. They are paddling across a loch. They use short paddles with two flat ends to make the boat go the right way. Each person is wearing a big orange jacket.

Cameron reads about learning to paddle, turning and stopping. He also reads about the jacket. It is a life jacket. If you fall in it stops you drowning.

He imagines paddling a little blue canoe down an exciting river with rocks in it. In the bottom of the canoe there is a bag of food and a box of matches. The matches are to light a fire when he stops for lunch.

Cameron writes on his piece of paper 'Raasay House is a really cool outdoor centre. It is far away. It is in the far North of Scotland. You can go canoeing and make big fires.'

"Louise," he says, "I'm very happy that we are going for a week."

Chapter 3 Driving to Raasay

Louise gets up very early on the day the children leave for Raasay. She wants to feed her hamster and say goodbye to the cat before it is time to go. She walks to school with her big sister, Carol. Carol helps her carry her bag.

"Why is it so heavy?" asks Carol.

"Food," says Louise.

Carol laughs. "Do you think there is no food on Raasay?" she asks.

"It's for the midnight feast," says Louise.

She has brought sweets, crisps and chocolate.

"That will be a good midnight feast," says Carol.

Cameron arrives at the school at the same time as Louise. His mum gave him a lift on the way to her work. Cameron takes his bag quickly and jumps out of the car.

"Bye, Mum," he shouts.

"Text me!" she calls back.

Cameron's bag is very big and has wheels.

"What have you got in there?" asks Louise. "Have you brought food for the midnight feast too?"

Cameron looks surprised. "Was I supposed to bring food?"

"It's OK," says Louise, "you can have some of mine."

"Did you remember to bring your lunch?" says Louise.

"Yes," says Cameron. My Mum made it. "She gave me Irn Bru!" he says to Louise. "She does not usually let me have it."

While Louise and Cameron are talking some other children arrive and stand near them. Then the coach comes round the corner.

At eleven o'clock the coach is driving between really high mountains. Louise and Cameron are sitting together on the bus. They are looking out of the window.

"Do you think there are any haggis up there?" asks Louise.

"What?" says Cameron.

"You know, haggis. Little hairy animals with one leg longer than the other. They run round mountains."

Just then Mrs MacDonald is walking down the bus. She hears what they say. She laughs. "That is just a story," she says.

"You mean it's not true!" says Louise. "My uncle told me about them when I came to live in Glasgow."

"That is because you came from England," says Mrs MacDonald. "The Scots tell the English these stories. It's a joke."

Mrs MacDonald starts to tell them her story.

"I lived in England before I came to live in Scotland. I thought it was a wild and wet place with lots of mountains. When I got the job in Glasgow I did not know what it would be like. I thought I would see hairy, redheaded Scotsmen in kilts running after haggis, when I was on the way to school. But there were only ordinary rows of houses and ordinary people. Maybe Raasay will be different."

Louise and Cameron look out the bus windows again. All they can see is steep hills. It is starting to rain.

"I'm so hungry," says Cameron.

"Again?" says Louise. "You have just had your lunch."

Most of the children have eaten all their lunch already. And a few of them have been sick too. Lots of children feel sick on buses. The road goes up and down and from side to side. It makes them feel worse.

The teacher stands up at the front of the bus. "Soon we are going to stop in Fort William. You can get off the bus and walk around the town. Then it will be two more hours to the Skye Bridge."

What a long trip!

"Do you think I can buy some food in Fort William?" says Cameron.

Much later they are near the Skye Bridge. When Louise looks out the window she can just see the road go up high in the distance. "Mum told me about the Skye Bridge last

night," says Cameron. "There was a ferry to Skye before the bridge was here."

"It sounds much more exciting to go on a ferry," says Louise.

"It is good practice for canoeing and sailing," says Cameron.

"Almost there," says Louise as they drive off the bridge.

It is warm on the bus. Cameron had a meat pie in Fort William so he is not hungry any more. He sits back and closes his eyes.

Chapter 4 On the ferry to Raasay

Suddenly a loud noise wakes Cameron.

"What was that?"

Louise is looking out the window. Cameron looks too. The coach is driving onto a boat. It does not look like a boat. It is made of metal and there are lots of cars and lorries. The bus drives up a ramp. The coach drives onto the boat and stops.

There is a loud noise. Louise and Cameron turn around. Behind them the ramp is going up. It is not just a ramp; it is the back of the boat too.

"I wonder how that works?" says Louise.

Just then the teacher tells the children that they may get off the coach. They may walk around on the boat.

Louise and Cameron are very happy to stand up and move around. They were sitting on the bus for a long time. They feel fed up.

"Are we ever going to get there?" asks Cameron.

They look around the ferry. It is like a small car park. All the cars are parked very close together. Some drivers cannot open the doors of their cars.

Cameron looks at the coach. "How does the driver turn to drive off the boat onto the island?" he asks Louise.

"I don't know," says Louise. "How does the captain make sure the ferry is close enough to the island so that the cars can drive off? Does he make a mistake sometimes? Do some of the cars fall into the sea?"

"I hope that does not happen to the bus," answers Cameron.

They go over to look at the ramp. It is straight up now. The sea is on the other side. You can see the waves but they stay on the other side.

The children can see lots of big hills beyond the sea. They are mountains like the ones they drove between. They cannot see them very well because it's raining. There is a loud noise and the hills start to move round the boat. Cameron and Louise are a bit surprised. Then they see that the boat is moving, not the hills.

Cameron and Louise follow the other children up a small metal ladder. They are on a different part of the ferry now. They can see more. They can see the jetty. That is where the coach drove onto the ferry. There is a big concrete ramp. It starts to disappear into the distance. The ferry is moving across the sea between the hills.

All the children are up on the ferry now. They are looking at the hills, or looking for toilets or food. It is very cold.

"I'm very happy that I have my warm jacket on," says Cameron.

Soon they are close to the island. They see a different concrete ramp. There is a small building and few cars in a line near it. A voice comes through the loudspeaker on the boat.

It asks everyone to get back into the cars. They have to go back to the coach. They all climb in, just in time.

Cameron is surprised when the coach does not need to turn to drive onto the island. Suddenly the front of the ferry starts going down. This boat has a ramp at each end. All the cars start their engines and drive off. Very soon all the other buses, cars, vans and lorries have disappeared on the island roads. The school coach is still on the jetty.

The bus driver and the teacher are at the front of the bus. They are looking at a map trying to decide which way to go.

"We are on the Island of Raasay at last," says Louise.

Chapter 5 At Raasay House

The coach drives along near the sea. It goes past some very small white houses and a red telephone box. There is a little school and a shop too. They see an arrow to the youth hostel. Then the road goes up a hill and into a wood. When they come out of the trees it is still raining. The coach is at the end of a wide drive, and there is Raasay House!

It is so big! It looks just like the picture in the classroom, but much bigger. The coach stops and the children all sit there looking at it.

A tall woman in a long, bright dress comes out of the house. She opens the great big wooden doors. All the children get off the coach. They run through the rain to go in. She asks them all to stand still.

"Welcome to Raasay House!" she says. "My name is Kate. I am an instructor here." Then she tells them some rules. She tells them where they can go, when to go to bed, meals and other things.

Cameron is thinking: 'This is so boring! I want to look around'.

She tells them the story of the house too. No one is listening. They do not think this is interesting. They want to see they house.

In the end she counts them out into little groups. Each group is sent to a room.

"Kate has made a mistake," whispers Cameron to Louise. "She sent me in with Robbie, Ryan, and Connor. I don't know them very well!"

"Maybe you can make friends with them," says Louise. "Go and look at your room. See you back here in 10 minutes."

Louise disappears with the other girls. They are all talking.

Cameron's room is on the top floor. It is hard for him to get his bag up the narrow stairs. It is too wide and too big. The little wheels do not work on the stairs. When he reaches the room he is very cross.

The other boys are already sitting on the beds, eating Liquorice Allsorts. They are talking about the football teams they support. Cameron does not like football and he does not like Liquorice Allsorts.

"Well, are we going?" says Robbie.

"Yes," answers Ryan.

Then Connor says, "OK," and they all get up and go, leaving Cameron there alone.

"What about me?" thinks Cameron.

He gets his phone out to text his mum:

At R house. Really Gr8. c u next week

Then he starts unpacking his things slowly – alarm clock, pyjamas, toothbrush and … Piggy?

Cameron is happy to see his toy, Piggy. Piggy sleeps in his bed at home, but Cameron does not want the other boys to see him. He looks around for a place to hide him.

He looks between the bed and the wall. Piggy is too big. Cameron gets up and pulls the bed away from the wall. He puts his hand down the space. There is something there already – it is folded paper. Cameron looks at it quickly, it looks like a letter. He hides Piggy and keeps the letter. Then he goes to find Louise.

Chapter 6 Ghost stories by the fire

After dinner the children look for something to do. Some of them go into a big room with comfortable chairs and sofas. There is a log fire in the room. This is the first time Louise has seen a real fire. She watches the flames.

Then the lights go quickly on and off, like flashes. Everyone looks up. Then it is bright again.

Louise is still looking into the fire. Cameron is sitting near her. He wonders if there is a TV. Mrs MacDonald comes in. She starts to tell the children what they will be doing. She planned that they will play games in the big room.

The lights flash again, this time they do not go back on. It is very dark and quiet. The fire makes big shadows.

They hear the door open.

Kate comes in. "Don't worry," she says, "we have power cuts all the time. The lights will come on again soon. The cook has a gas stove; she will make hot chocolate for everyone. We have lots of wood. You will be warm enough here with the fire. I will get some candles and matches."

She disappears into the darkness.

Later she comes back with candles in jars. She lights the candles and puts them around the room. Mrs MacDonald comes in with the other children. She has been walking round the house with a big torch. She was looking for anyone lost in the dark.

Kate sits down near the fire. "I hope the candles don't start off the smoke alarm," she says. "That would give you a surprise! When it happened last time everyone thought it was a ghost."

"Do you have any ghosts at Raasay House?" asks a voice. Cameron thinks it is Ryan but he cannot see in the dark.

"Oh yes!" says Kate. "There are about forty rooms here. There is lots of space for ghosts!"

Duncan, one of the instructors comes in. He is carrying lots of cups with hot chocolate. "Oh good!" he says. "Are you telling ghost stories? Can I stay?"

Kate tells the children about the haunted graveyard. "It's behind the house. Some of you can see the little church from your rooms."

Kate says most of the ghosts are ordinary people. They lived in the house and village and were buried in that graveyard. But some of the ghosts are not ordinary. They are very tall. She says the first people who lived on Raasay were very big. Over 7 feet tall. They were put in very long graves. She says some nights all the ghosts at the graveyard have a ceilidh. That is a Scottish party with singing and dancing. They dance the *Dashing White Sergeant*.

"Can we have a ceilidh on the last night here?" asks Robbie. Mrs MacDonald thinks that is a good idea.

Kirsty wants to know if the ghosts speak Gaelic.

Gaelic is the language people used to speak in parts of Scotland. Kate says most people on Raasay can speak Gaelic and English.

"I think if the ghosts are from Raasay they will all speak Gaelic too," says Duncan.

"Does that make the ghosts more scary or not?" whispers Louise to Cameron.

"I don't know," says Cameron. "If the ghosts speak Gaelic you will not understand them."

"What do you do if you can understand them?"

"Shake hands and speak to them in Gaelic too!" laughs Louise.

"Have you told them about the ghost dogs?" says Duncan. He is sitting on the floor in the corner of the room. There are no candles near him and his voice comes out of the dark.

He begins to tell them about the big Scottish deerhounds that haunt the house. The MacLeod family used to have very big pets. When they were dead they put them in a special graveyard for pets, near the walled garden. "They only come when you are ill in bed so I hope you don't see them," he says, "they are so big they can see you even if you are in the top bunk."

"You can see the ghosts of Boswell and Johnson," says Kate.

"Are they dogs too?" asks Cameron.

"No," says Louise, "you did not listen at school. They are famous people. They came to Raasay House a long time ago."

Kate tells them that the bedroom Boswell and Johnson stayed in is haunted by Johnson.

He appears there in a big white shirt and long riding boots. He writes his diary at the desk. Cameron wants to ask which bedroom it is. Just then the lights flash and come on again.

Mrs MacDonald gets up. "Come on everyone," she says, "time for bed."

It takes a long time but in the end all the children go to bed. They are all making ghost noises on the way to their rooms.

Chapter 7 Canoeing

The next morning it is not raining. It is bright and clear. After breakfast the next day the children are all waiting in front of the house. Mrs MacDonald asks them to stand in a long line. She walks all the way along the line giving each child a number.

"One, two, three, one, two, three."

At the end she stops and looks back. "Everyone who is number one," she says, "is going canoeing today. Number two: abseiling. Number three: kayaking."

Louise is in the abseiling group. Cameron is going canoeing.

The canoeing group starts by taking most of their clothes off! They put on wetsuits. Then they put their trainers back on their feet. The instructor gives each child a life jacket. It looks like the ones on the website. It is very big. Kirsty is in Cameron's group. She is very small. The life jacket looks bigger than she is.

The canoes are on a trailer. Duncan, the instructor, sends the children over to the trailer in groups of four. Each group must take down a canoe and bring it to the water. The canoes are very big but not very heavy.

Soon all the canoes are on the beach. They start to take them into the loch. The children must walk into the loch. They all look at each other. No one wants to step into the cold water. At last Robbie splashes into the loch. At first he feels nothing. Then the cold water starts to come in through his trainers. It is very cold. He waits for it to start to come up his legs too but it does not. The wet suit keeps him dry. Only his feet are wet.

The other children stand by the loch and watch. Robbie turns round. "Come in! The water is lovely," he shouts and splashes them all. Soon all the children are splashing around in the water.

The instructors have to work hard to get all the children into groups and into their boats. They show them how to hold the boat while they climb in.

Cameron looks back up at Raasay House. He can see the kayaking group. They are on the ground in front of the house. Kayaks are small boats for one person only. The kayaks are in a circle on the ground in front of the house. The children sit in them and practice paddling.

At last there are four canoes in the loch, each with four children in it. Duncan is in a different canoe. Kate comes running down from the house. She has her own canoe. She jumps in and paddles it out next to Duncan.

Duncan tells the children again about safety. He tells them to stay together.

Kirsty is very worried about falling in. She asks what to do if she falls in. Duncan suggests they try it! All the children start try to make the canoes fall over. This is hard. The boats stay the right way up. The children move from side to side but the canoes still don't fall over. Duncan gets out of his canoe and walks over to Cameron's canoe. "I will give you a hand," he says and gives their boat a big push.

Splash!

Cameron's canoe is on its side in the water. The four children are in the water. They are all floating because they are wearing life jackets. The children cannot swim but they are all floating. Cameron likes floating in the loch in his wet suit. He feels warm under his wet suit and life jacket!

"See!" he calls to Kirsty, "if you fall in, you can have a lovely float."

Duncan helps them to put the boat the right way up and helps them all get back in. Now they are ready to learn to use the paddles and take the canoes for a trip around the loch.

On a different part of Raasay, near Brochel castle, Louise puts on special boots for abseiling. On the ground near her is a harness to wear and a helmet to keep her head safe.

Chapter 8 Lunchtime

When the children meet at lunchtime they all have stories to tell. The canoeing group have taken off their wetsuits and put their clothes on again. They are wearing dry shoes too. The abseiling group has had a very exciting time. They want to tell the others how they did it.

Ryan says it was scary before he tried it. "I got to the top and looked down. It was a very long way. All I could see was dangerous rocks."

"Yes," says Louise, "it was scary, but exciting too. I was too frightened to start. The first step was the worst. Then it went really fast. Half way down I stopped to look round at everything."

"It was over so quickly," says a boy called Gordon, "I climbed back up and did it all again!"

Connor was in the kayaking group. He is very excited because they saw a family of three otters.

"That is nothing," says Robbie, "we saw a Raasay vole! That is a sort of mouse that only lives on Raasay."

"What did it look like?" asks Kirsty.

"Just like a mouse really," answers Robbie with a laugh! "It did not have 'Made in Raasay' written on its back!"

"Abseiling makes you really hungry," says Ryan. "Let's eat!"

"Oh no!" shouts Louise. "I forgot my lunch pack."

Cameron laughs at the look on her face. "You can have half of mine," he says.

Some of the girls give her a bit of their lunch too. In the end she has more food than any of the others.

"You can stay here and do nothing for an hour," says Duncan after lunch. "We will be going orienteering later. Maybe there will be time to climb Dun Caan too. It's the biggest mountain on Raasay."

"Don't run off!" he says and lies down on the heather.

Louise lies down on the heather too. The sun is warm.

"What did you think of the ghost stories last night?" asks Cameron.

"I think Kate and Duncan made them up," says Louise.

Cameron is looking for more food. He cannot find any food but here is the letter he found behind his bed.

"Oh, I forgot, Louise. I found this behind my bed."

He shows her the letter. She looks at it but does not touch it.

"Why did you bring that? It must be some rubbish hidden behind the bed."

Cameron starts to open it up. Louise is right. Maybe it is something horrible – someone's used chewing gum ... or worse. But he carries on. It is one piece of folded paper. It is not dirty. There is writing on the front and the back. Someone's diary? No, it is a letter.

There is no date or address at the top of the letter. Cameron and Louise look at the letter together and read it.

Dear Friend,
Have you just arrived at Raasay House? Was it raining on the ferry? It usually is.
You are sleeping in my old bed I want to tell you some secrets about Raasay House ...

This sounds strange and interesting. They hope it will tell them about the ghosts.

But the letter is not strange and interesting. It is all about food. The writer's favourite food is beef olives, fish and chips, lamb casserole and curry. He says the cook at Raasay House is very good at making them all. The letter also says that the best puddings are millionaire's shortbread or apple pie with ice cream.

> *Do not eat the custard; it is always burnt.*
> *If you feel hungry at night have a midnight feast. It is easy to break in to the kitchen for food. All you have to do …*

Then there are long, careful instructions about getting into the kitchen when the door is locked at night. Cameron reads the instructions carefully and tries to remember them. They will help if Louise runs out of food.

> *Be careful in the dark at Raasay House. You never know what you will meet.*
> *Do not use the last one in the row in the downstairs toilets.*

Cameron and Louise look at each other. A ghost? A monster?

Cameron is already imagining a horrible Gaelic monster coming to bite his bottom on the toilet.

They turn the page …

> *… Don't use that one because it does not flush very well!*

Chapter 9 The Cave

Duncan is sleeping on the heather. The children have had enough of doing nothing.

"I want to go and have a look around now," says Cameron.

Louise gets to her feet.

"Can we come?" say Ryan, Connor and Robbie.

Kirsty is standing near Louise, ready to go.

The six children start walking towards the trees near the loch. They go into the forest. It is dark and a bit wet. There is a path between the trees. The children follow the path. It goes round a big rock and up a hill. It is very narrow. The children walk in single file.

Kirsty is at the end. She drops her bag. When she stops to get it the other children are far away. "Wait for me!" she shouts.

The children get to the top of the little hill.

"Where is the path?" says Cameron.

The path has gone. They don't want to go back the same way. They climb down the hill a different way. They begin to run. They all arrive at the bottom laughing.

Ryan is looking at the hill. There is a big crack in the rock. It is just wider than Ryan. Without a word he starts to climb in. Kirsty sees him.

"Where are you going? Come back! I think it is dangerous!" she calls.

Ryan does not hear her, or does not want to. He disappears into the cave. The other children go over and look into the crack in the rock. One by one, they follow him inside. Cameron and Louise are last.

When they are all in it is very dark. Cameron puts his hand out in the dark. He feels a cold, wet wall. Then he finds Louise. He puts his hand on her arm. The children are whispering. The cave sounds very big.

"How big is it?" he asks.

Someone answers that he does not know.

"We could try feeling along the walls," says a different voice.

"We must stay together," says Kirsty. "Everyone should hold hands."

The children feel around in the dark to find each other. They start to scream and laugh when they touch each other. Suddenly they hear something. They all stop. Was that a voice? There it is again!

"Ciamar a tha thu," says the voice. All the children move to stand very close together.

"Ciamar a tha thu," it says again. The children are too frightened to speak.

"Glè mhath," says the voice.

"How can we get out?" whispers Connor. He sounds very frightened.

"I know how," whispers Louise, "I can see the light." All the children are holding on to each other. They move towards Louise. She walks them slowly towards the light. They are still very quiet.

"Glè mhath!" says the voice again. *"Sassenach!"* it calls. The voice sounds much nearer now.

After a very long time they get to the crack. No one wants to be first out and no one wants to be last out. Kirsty and Ryan go out first. Cameron is last. The other children pull him quickly through the crack. The children are all standing outside the cave staring at each other. Their faces are very white.

"That was a close shave," says Ryan, "it almost got us."

"Ciamar a tha thu, Sassenach !" says the voice.

It sounds very loud and very close.

"It followed us!" says Robbie in alarm.

There is a flash of colour. Blue and red. A big parrot flies over and sits on Ryan's head. Ryan screams and jumps. The parrot moves away. He is looking at the children. *"Ciamar a tha thu !"* he shouts. They are all looking at the Gaelic parrot in surprise.

"Sassenach!" it says.

Robbie knows what to do. His grandfather has a parrot.

He goes over and puts out his arm to the parrot. It moves over to stand on his arm. The parrot is very quiet. "Let's take it back and ask for a translation," says Robbie. All the children laugh. The parrot shakes its feathers.

Chapter 10 The Find

There is no orienteering this afternoon. All the children get back into the boats and take the parrot back to Raasay House. It sits on the front of Robbie's canoe.

"You better not capsize," says Duncan. "Your passenger is not wearing a life jacket."

Kate looks at them in surprise when they all arrive early at Raasay House carrying a large noisy parrot. She knows the parrot.

"Hello, Hamish!" she says. "You are a bad bird! Have you flown away again?"

"*Sassenach!*" says Hamish.

"Would you like to phone Donald?" says Kate, laughing. "Or will I do it for you?"

Before very long the children can hear a car on the road outside the house. A big van drives up and two people jump out. One of them is Donald. Hamish flies over to him and sits on his arm.

"*Ciamar a tha thu,*" says Hamish

"*Glè mhath,*" answers Donald.

Donald tells the children that Hamish often flies away but this time he has been missing for three weeks. "I thought he had left the Island," says Donald. He turns to the parrot and says, "I thought you wanted to live in Glasgow."

Donald tells them that *Ciamar a tha thu* means 'How are you?' – *Glè mhath,* is the answer. It means 'Very well'.

"What about *Sassenach*?" asks Kirsty.

"That means 'lowlander'," says Donald. "Scottish people sometimes call English people *Sassenach*."

"… and so do Scottish parrots!" says Robbie with a laugh.

Then Donald turns to the other man. "This is James Harris," he says. "I don't have a car so James gave me a lift. James lives near me. He is also the photographer of the island newspaper."

"Can I take a picture of you for the newspaper?" James asks the children.

The children like the idea very much.

It takes James a long time to arrange all the children, Mrs MacDonald and the instructors on the steps of Raasay House for the photograph. When he is nearly ready he says, "OK, bring out Hamish."

But where is Hamish? Everyone looks at each other and then begins to look around.

"Oh, no!" says Donald. "Not again!"

"There he is," says Cameron looking at the van. Hamish is sitting on the steering wheel. "I think he wants to go home."

Donald goes over to fetch him. "Come on, Hamish!" he says. "We can go home soon, after your photograph."

"*Glè mhath,*" says Hamish.

A Ghost in the Cave: An Adventure on Raasay Island

by our correspondent James Harris

After a morning of many different outdoor activities six children from Raasay House start walking towards the trees near the loch. They go into the forest. It is dark and a bit wet. There is a path between the trees. The children follow the path. It goes round a big rock and up a hill. It is very narrow. The children walk in single file. The children get to the top of the little hill.

The path has gone. They don't want to go back the same way. They climb down the hill a different way. They begin to run. They all arrive at the bottom laughing.

Ryan is looking at the hill. There is a big crack in the rock. It is just wider than Ryan. Without a word he starts to climb in. He disappears into the cave. The other children go over and look into the crack in the rock. One by one, they follow him inside. Cameron and Louise are last.

When they are all in it is very dark. Cameron puts his hand out in the dark. He feels a cold, wet wall. Then he finds Louise. He puts his hand on her arm. The children are whispering. The cave sounds very big. The children feel around in the dark to find each other. They start to scream and laugh when they touch each other. Suddenly they hear something. They all stop. Was that a voice? There it is again! All the children move to stand very close together because they are frightened.

'I know how to get out of here, 'whispers Louise, 'I can see the light'. All the children are holding on to each other. They move towards Louise.She walks them slowly towards the light. They are still very quiet.

After a very long time they get to the crack. No one wants to be first out and no one wants to be last out. Kirsty and Ryan go out first. Cameron is last. The

Vocabulary

Chapter 1

exciting aufregend
announcement Ankündigung
parrot Papagei
Prime Minister [ˌpraɪm 'mɪnɪstə] Premier Minister von GB
ferry (Fahrzeug-/ Personen)Fähre
everyone jeder
exciting aufregend
outdoor draußen, im Freien
canoeing [kə'nuːɪŋ] Kanufahren
orienteering [ˌɔːriən'tɪərɪŋ] Orientierungslauf
abseiling ['æbseɪlɪŋ] sich abseilen
sailing ['seɪlɪŋ] Segeln, Segelsport
kayaking ['kaɪækɪŋ] Kayakfahren
difference Unterschied
cliff [klɪf] Klippe
mainland Festland
Missus ['mɪsɪs] *(dialect)* Mrs ['mɪsɪz]
instructors Ausbilder/innen
far too bei weitem
excited aufgeregt

Chapter 2

maps Landkarten
deer Rotwild
secondary school höhere Schule
capital Hauptstadt
arrow Pfeil
bonnie, bonny *(Scottish)* schön, hübsch
(to be) **fed up** genug haben
bigger than größer als
narrow schmal
at the back hinten
across a loch über einen See
loch [lɒk, lɒx] *(Scottish)* See
flat flach
(to) **drown** [draʊn] ertrinken
rocks Felsen
matches Streichhölzer
fire Feuer

Chapter 3

midnight feast Mitternachtsgelage
lift Mitfahrgelegenheit
Irn Bru ['aɪənbruː] *eine schottische koffeinhaltige Limonade, verkauft sich in Schottland besser als Coca Cola*
coach Reisebus
haggis *schottische Spezialität, vergleichbar mit dem Saumagen*
wet nass, feucht
hairy behaart
rows Reihen
steep steil
(to be) **sick** sich übergeben
(to) **feel sick** Übelkeit empfinden
worse [wɜːs] schlechter
(to) **drive off** herunterfahren

meat pie Fleischpastete, Fleischtasche

Chapter 4

noise Geräusch
lots of lorries viele Lastwagen
ramp Rampe
get off aussteigen
(to) **move around** (sich) hin und her bewegen
straight up gerade aufgerichtet
jetty ['dʒeti] Mole, Hafendamm, Landebrücke
concrete Beton

Chapter 5

hostel Herberge
wood Wald
(to) **count them out into groups** nach Gruppen abzählen
(to) **disappear** verschwinden
(to be) **cross** verärgert
Liquorice Allsorts [ˌlɪkərɪʃ 'ɔːlsɔːts] *bunte Lakritzemischung*
space (Zwischen)Raum
folded gefaltet

Chapter 6

log Holzscheit
like flashes wie ein Blinken
power cuts Stromausfälle
gas stove ['gæs stəʊv] Gasherd
candles Kerzen
jars (Marmeladen)Gläser
torch Taschenlampe
smoke alarm Rauchmelder
surprise Überraschung
ghost Geist, Gespenst
haunted graveyard Friedhof, auf dem es spukt
buried beerdigt
7 feet tall über 2 m groß (1 foot = 30,48 cm)
graves Gräber
Ceilidh ['keɪli] *traditioneller gälischer Gesellschaftstanz*
Gaelic ['gælɪk, 'geɪlɪk] Gälische Sprache der Schotten
deerhound schottischer Hirschhund
haunt the house [hɔːnt] im Haus spuken
even sogar
top bunk oberstes Etagenbett
famous berühmt
Boswell and Johnson:
Samuel Johnson *(1709–1784) englischer Gelehrter*
James Boswell *(1740–1795) Biograph von S. Johnson*
riding boots Reitstiefel

Chapter 7

wetsuit ['wetsuːt] Neoprenanzug zum Schwimmen/Surfen etc.
trainers Turnschuhe
life jacket Schwimmweste
trailer Anhänger
(to) **splash** Spritzen, Platschen
floating treibend
float Herumtreiben
harness Ausrüstung *hier:* Klettergeschirr
helmet Helm

Chapter 8

has had hatte gehabt
worst [wɜːst] am schlimmsten
fast schnell
otters Fischotter
vole Mühlmaus
rubbish Müll, Mist
hidden versteckt
address Adresse
beef olives *eine Art Rindsrouladen*
lamb [læm] Lamm
shortbread *schottisches Mürbeteiggebäck*
custard ['kʌstəd] englische Vanillesoße
bottom *(hier)* Hintern, Po
(to) **flush** [flʌʃ] spülen

Chapter 9

heather Heide(kraut)
hill Hügel
single file Gänsemarsch
crack Felsspalte
(to) **climb** [klaɪm] in hineinklettern
(to) **scream** kreischen
Ciamar a tha thu [kjimar a haː u] *(Gaelic)*
frightened erschrocken, verängstigt
Glè mhath ['gleː vah] *(Gaelic)*
Saasenach ['sæsənæk, sasə'nəx] *(Gaelic)* Engländer (eigentlich „Sachse“)
translation Übersetzung
feathers Federn

Chapter 10

(to) capsize [kæp'saɪz] kentern
noisy laut
Have you flown away again? Bist du wieder weggeflogen?
I thought he had left the island. Ich dachte, er hätte die Insel verlassen.
steering wheel Lenkrad

Names and Place Names

Aberdeen [ˌæbə'diːn]
Andrew ['ændruː]
Boswell ['bɒzwəl]
Brochel Castle ['brɒkəl]
Cameron ['kæmərən]
Campbell ['kæmbəl]
Carol ['kærəl]
Connor ['kɒnə]
Donald ['dɒnəld]
Duncan ['dʌŋkən]
Fiona [fi'əʊnə]
Fort William [ˌfɔːt 'wɪljəm]
Glasgow ['glɑːzgəʊ]
Gordon ['gɔːdn]
Hamish ['heɪmɪʃ]
Inverness [ˌɪnvə'nes]
Johnson ['dʒɒnsən]
Kirsty ['kɜːsti]
Louise [luː'iːz]
McCracken [mə'krækən]
MacDonald [mək'dɒnəld]
MacLeod [mə'klaʊd]
Neil [nɪəl]
Portree [pɔː'triː]
Raasay ['rɑːseɪ]
Rory ['rɔːri]
Ryan ['raɪən]
Skye [skaɪ]

Questions and Activities

Chapter 1

1 On the Scottish island something has gone missing. What is it?

2 When the door of the classroom in Glasgow opens the children hope it will be someone exciting. Who would you like to visit you? Draw a picture and write a few words about that person.

3 Where will the children stay on the school trip? How will it be different from home?

4 The story says a letter will be sent to the parents giving more information. Write down some of the things that should be in the letter.

Chapter 2

1 Describe the exercise Mrs MacDonald has set the children.

2 What has Louise learnt about Raasay? Write down three things.

3 Cameron is looking at a picture of canoeing on the computer. Read the description and try to draw the picture.

4 Look at the map of Scotland. Cameron is looking at Aberdeen and Inverness. He cannot see Skye, Raasay or Raasay House. Why?

   a He is not wearing his glasses.
   b They are not on the map.
   c This is not a map of Scotland.
   d He is looking in the wrong place.

5 Write down what you find on the Raasay House website. What do you like best?

Chapter 3

1 Why does Louise get up early?

2 What does Louise want to eat in the night?

3 Read the description of the haggis running round the hill. Can you draw it? You might find some pictures to help you in books or on the Internet.

Chapter 4

1 The bus drives onto the ferry to Raasay. Then the ramp closes behind the bus. When they arrive at Raasay the ramp at the front of the ferry comes down and the bus drives off. This is a roll-on roll-off ferry. These ferries take cars and buses to islands all over Scotland. Draw a series of 3 or 4 pictures to show how a roll-on roll-off ferry works.

2 What is missing? Find the words in the text.

a The ferry is made of ....

b The ferry is like a small ....

c Cameron and Louise go up a small metal ....

d The children on the ferry are looking for .... and ....

3 On jetties in Scotland there is a road sign telling drivers not to drive off the edge *(Rand)*, into the sea. Draw a road sign that would tell drivers to be careful near the sea.

Chapter 5

1 Cameron had written a text message to his mum. It is not exactly true. What do you think he might write to his brother?
2 Why does Cameron not want the boys to see Piggy?
3 When Cameron leaves Raasay House at the end of the holiday he forgets to pack Piggy. Next day he phones Kate to ask her to look for him and post him to Glasgow. Write a short dialogue of the phone conversation and act it out.

Chapter 6

1 Why does Kate put the candles into jars?
2 Read the description of the ghosts and draw them having a ceilidh at night.
3 The ghosts dance the *Dashing White Sergeant*. Your class can learn a Scottish dance. Maybe you can find a Scottish person to teach you? You can look in a book or find help on the Internet.
4 Johnson wrote a diary of his stay in Raasay house. Write a short piece for a diary of a day there.

Chapter 7

1 Choose someone to be the teacher. That person should split up the children into groups as Mrs. MacDonald does.

Group one	–	canoeing
Group two	–	abseiling
Group three	–	kayaking

2 Each group reads through the description of their activity and act it out. You can use the English dialogue in the story and add some of your own.

Chapter 8

1 The letter writer is very interested in food. Talk about your favourite food in class and try to describe them in English.
2 How do you think you might get into the kitchen if the door is locked?
3 The children have seen otters and Raasay voles. Try to find out what other animals they might see in the Scottish countryside.

Chapter 9

Six children go exploring into the cave. Split up into groups of 4–6. Make up a story about going into a cave and finding something strange. Act it out. Use the language in the story and other words you know the children might say.
Each group can act out their scene for the others.

Chapter 10

1 Why does the parrot speak Gaelic?
2 Do you think it can understand Gaelic too?
3 Dou you think it can understand English?
4 Write a short article to go with the photograph in the local newspaper.

Solution Chapter 4/2

a metal; b car park; c ladder; d toilets and food

Scottish items: Interesting & entertaining information for teachers to pass on to class

Title

Isle of Raasay

http://www.raasay.com/

http://en.wikipedia.org/wiki/Raasay

Raasay House

http://www.raasayoutdoorcentre.co.uk/

Chapter 2

Bonnie Prince Charlie Prinz Charles Edward Stuart, der den englischen Thron für die königliche Familie der Stuarts gegen die Engländer zurück gewinnen wollte

http://de.wikipedia.org/wiki/Charles_Edward_Stuart

Chapter 3

Irn Bru eine schottische koffeinhaltige Limonade, verkauft sich in Schottland besser als Coca Cola

http://de.wikipedia.org/wiki/Irn-Bru

Chapter 4

haggis schottische Spezialität, vergleichbar mit dem pfälzischen Saumagen

http://de.wikipedia.org/wiki/Haggis

Chapter 5

Liquorice Allsorts bunte Lakritzemischung

http://en.wikipedia.org/wiki/Liquorice_allsorts

Chapter 6

Ceilidh traditioneller gälischer Gesellschaftstanz
http://www.highland-bagpipe.com/ceilidhdance.htm
http://www.geocities.com/Colosseum/Midfield/3705/DashingWhiteSergeant.htm
Gaelic Gälische Sprache der Schotten
http://de.wikipedia.org/wiki/Schottisch-G%C3%A4lische_Sprache
http://en.wikipedia.org/wiki/Gaelic
Boswell and Johnson
Samuel Johnson (1709–1784) englischer Gelehrter
James Boswell (1740–1795) Biograph von Samuel Johnson
http://yalepress.yale.edu/yupbooks/book.asp?isbn=0300052103

Chapter 8

Beef olives Rindsrouladen
http://www.bbc.co.uk/food/recipes/database/beefolives_68.shtml
shortbread schottisches Mürbeteiggebäck
http://de.wikipedia.org/wiki/Shortbread
millionaire's shortbread
http://uktv.co.uk/index.cfm/uktv/food.recipe/aid/516853
Raasay vole Wühlmaus, die nur in Raasay vorkommt
http://en.wikipedia.org/wiki/Raasay
custard englische Vanillesoße
http://www.blogigo.de/ostwestwind/Custard-versus-Vanillesosse/90/

Chapter 9

Sassenach (Scottish) Engländer (eigentlich „Sachse")
http://en.wikipedia.org/wiki/Sassenach

Alle Webseiten geprüft 2007